To Daddy from Tess.

THE BRITISH COMMONWEALTH IN PICTURES

CANADA

GENERAL EDITOR
W. J. TURNER

The General Editor is most grateful to all those who have so kindly helped in the selection of illustrations, especially to officials of the various public Museums, Libraries and Galleries, and to all others who have generously allowed pictures and MSS. to be reproduced

CANADA

LADY TWEEDSMUIR

With
twelve plates in colour
and thirty-two illustrations in
black and white

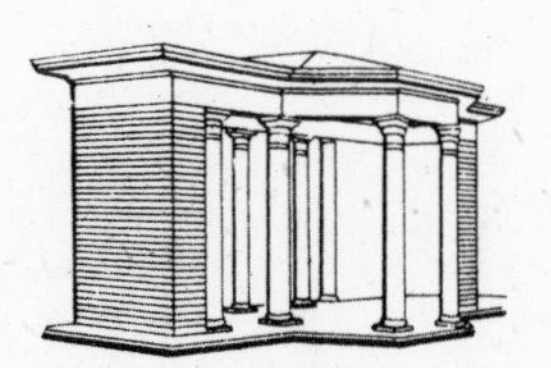

WILLIAM COLLINS OF LONDON

FIRST EDITION 1941
REPRINTED 1943

PRODUCED BY ADPRINT LONDON
PRINTED IN GREAT BRITAIN

LIST OF ILLUSTRATIONS

PLATES IN COLOUR

BLACK AND WHITE ILLUSTRATIONS

Illustrations on pp. 7, 9, 12, 13, 14, 23, 39 *are reproduced by courtesy of the British Museum: on pp.* 15, 22 *by courtesy of the Parker Gallery, London: on p.* 17 *by courtesy of Bernard Quaritch, Ltd., London: on pp.* 19, 27 *by courtesy of the Canadian Pacific Railway: on pp.* 28, 29 *by courtesy of Leggatt Bros., London: on p.* 26 *by courtesy of the Office of the High Commissioner for Canada and of the Royal Canadian Air Force: on pp.* 30, 31, 35, 36, 37, 41, 43 *by courtesy of the Office of the High Commissioner for Canada: on pp.* 32, 33, 34 *by courtesy of the photographer H. G. Casparius: on p.* 38 *by courtesy of the National Gallery of Canada: on pp.* 44, 45 *by courtesy of the artist and of the National Gallery of Canada: on pp.* 46, 47 *by courtesy of the Rt. Hon. Viscount Bennett.*

BRIEF HISTORICAL CHRONOLOGY

- *c.* 1000 CANADA probably reached by LEIF ERICSSON on an expedition from Greenland
- *c.* 1497 Discovered by JOHN CABOT sailing from Bristol
- *c.* 1534 JACQUES CARTIER, sent out by FRANCIS I of France, entered the Gulf of St. Lawrence
- *c.* 1535 CARTIER reached the spot where Montreal now stands
- *c.* 1604 SAMUEL DE CHAMPLAIN founded the French Colony of Port Royal, Nova Scotia
- *c.* 1629 An ENGLISH FLEET appeared at Quebec
- *c.* 1666 A FRENCH MISSION founded on shores of Lake Superior
- *c.* 1713 Hudson Bay, Newfoundland and Nova Scotia became BRITISH
- *c.* 1759 GENERAL WOLFE captured Quebec
- *c.* 1763 CANADA ceded to GREAT BRITAIN by France
- *c.* 1840 The Union of UPPER and LOWER CANADA
- *c.* 1867 CANADA becomes a Federal State
- *c.* 1926 CANADA becomes a member of the BRITISH COMMONWEALTH OF NATIONS

VIEW OF THE RIVER SAINT LAWRENCE
Water colour by John Townsend *c.* 1840

PREFACE.

IT is necessary for anyone who wishes to understand a country first to study her history, and Canada's history is a very interesting study. The two dominating factors which have produced the Canada of to-day are human courage and endurance, and the geography of this vast and marvellous land, which stretches from the Maritime Provinces to the Pacific coast. It is a saga of man's adventurous spirit in the face of every kind of hardship, and a salute to two great races, the British and the French, who began the conquest of Canada by force, and have maintained that conquest in years of peace.

In this sketch I cannot do more than glance at the sequence of events, and my hope is that the readers of this little book will be fired to study Canadian history in greater detail. It will well repay them so to do.

At this moment all eyes are turned upon the New World. Canadians have come once again, for the third time in forty years, to fight by our side. Surely it is a good moment to study the roots of Canada's history, roots which sprang from our soil and from the soil of France.

I have tried to show the special charm and flavour of each of those nine provinces which go to make up the Dominion of Canada. If I have succeeded in making their varied beauty and their varied interests a little more generally known, I shall feel amply rewarded.

S. T.

I.

THE BACKGROUND OF CANADA.

CANADA was first discovered and her settlement begun as the result of Marco Polo's discovery of China in the reigns of the first and second Edwards, Kings of England. The tale of the amazing civilisation of Cathay had made merchants of Spain, England, and the Italian Republic hungry for trade with the rich and prosperous East. In May 1497, John Cabot, an Italian from Bristol, fitted out a tiny ship, with a little help from King Henry VII, and sailed for North America.

He returned in July saying that he had reached land and planted a huge cross on the shore. He added that he had, without doubt, found the land of the Great Khan, and had also been very near Japan. He was made much of, and walked about clothed in silk, and was lavish in promises of the wealth to be gathered in the New World. A year later he sailed with two ships, and returned with tales of fishing and fur trading. After this England claimed the discovery of North America.

Nearly forty years later, in 1534, the French, who had heard the gossip of fishermen about North America, decided not to allow Spain and England to have this new continent, and Francis I chose Jacques Cartier, a hardy sailor from St. Malo, to sail on this great adventure. Cartier made a surprisingly fast voyage of three weeks, and reached the mouth of the St. Lawrence at the Strait of Belle Isle. Coasting along New Brunswick to Gaspé he sailed up an inlet. The day was very hot, and he named the inlet Baie de Chaleur. (Four hundred years later I passed along its shores when the temperature was below zero and the snow lay deep on the landscape, and I wondered why it had been given that name.)

Jacques Cartier was convinced that this inlet led to the gorgeous East, but the Indians whom he met seemed extremely poor and offered only one commodity, furs. At Gaspé Cartier planted a great wooden cross, and nailed on it a shield bearing the fleur-de-lys and a large scroll on which was written, "Vive le Roy."

The French conquest of Canada seems to have been a source of surprise and disappointment; surprise at the beauty and vastness of the country, and disappointment at the different life the explorers found there from that of their expectations. They came upon poor Indian villages surrounded by a triple palisade of logs, when they expected round the turn of the next hill or river to be gladdened by the sight of stately temples, groves of fruit, men and women dressed in exotic silks, and all the panoply of an old and wealthy civilisation. (La Chine rapids near Montreal were so called because French adventurers hoped just beyond them to find China in all her glory.) It was a dream that died hard, both in France and in England.

Cartier spent two years in Canada, then sailed back to France, taking with him an Indian chief. Reports went to Spain that Francis I was fitting out an

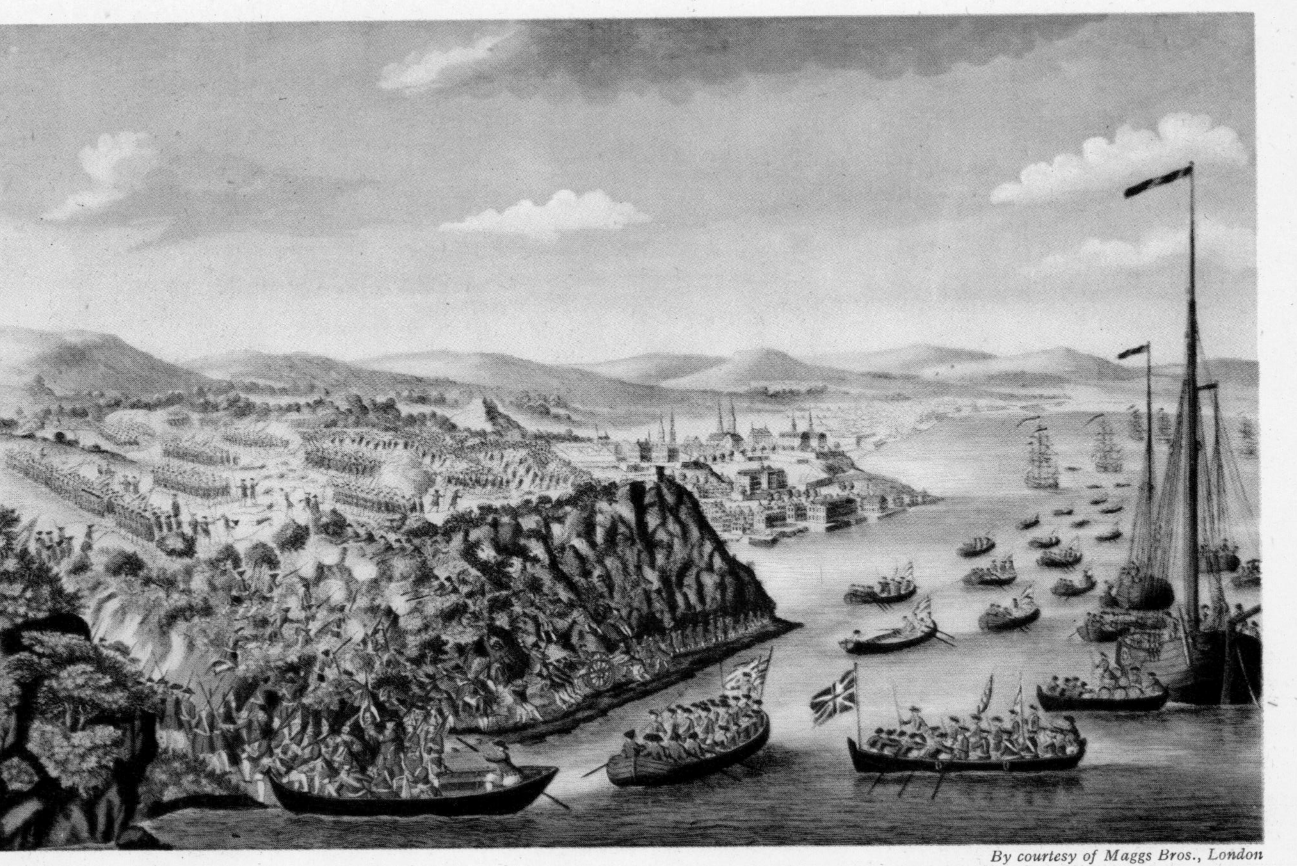

By courtesy of Maggs Bros., London

A VIEW OF THE TAKING OF QUEBEC, SEPTEMBER 13TH 1759
Coloured line engraving c.1790

By courtesy of Maggs Bros., London

CAPE DIAMOND AND WOLF'S COVE FROM POINT A PIZEAU

Coloured aquatint engraving by C. Hunt from the drawing by Lt.-Col. Cockburn

MAP OF CANADA *c.* 1544
Attributed to Desceliers
The picture is supposed to represent Jacques Cartier meeting the chief Donna Conna on the banks of the river opposite Quebec, on September 15th, 1535

expedition which was to colonise a new France. The Spaniards and Portuguese said that as long as the French did not take any of the land which belonged to them they might go to the chill North ; from which it was probably hoped that they would never return alive.

Five years after his first attempt Cartier landed again in Canada, still hoping to discover diamonds. He returned with no precious stones, but with some specimens of gold and crystals which had been found at Charlesbourg near Quebec.

The roll of honour of Canadian history is a fascinating study. Few countries have been served by men of such a highly adventurous spirit, and of such diverse characteristics. After Cartier the sailor and explorer, Champlain is the next great name. He was fervently religious and had patience, courage and tact. He needed all these qualities, as the French, like other colonists, were hard to manage, and the Indian tribes were both ruthless and formidable. The support which he had received from France was variable and capricious. He was a much travelled man, having penetrated into Mexico, and he made drawings and maps wherever he went. He has been blamed for allying himself with the

Indian tribes of Hurons and Algonquins, for although he gained some successes with their help, a century of bitter animosity with the Iroquois ensued. He explored as far as Lake Huron with a party of Indians, and was a long way from regarding the seaboard of Canada as the only place on which France should maintain her hold.

Meanwhile England had become interested in the fur trading which was going on in North America, and in 1622 sent out an expedition headed by Sir William Alexander, with a complete disregard of the fact that the French were already in occupation of part of Canada.

It is impossible in this short essay to go any further into the details of the complicated struggle between the French and the English. They sank each other's ships, and each tried to capture the valuable fishing and fur trade. In 1632 the French occupied Quebec, and Champlain, after thirty years of hard toil, saw trade flourish and emigrants arrive. He was the only man sent out by France who tried to establish farming and turn a trading colony into a permanent home for Frenchmen. His vision, courage and firmness made him perhaps the greatest figure in Canada's history. He crossed the Atlantic, with all its dangers, eight times, a very considerable achievement in itself in those days. He was one of the first of Empire builders, one of that company of men who, like Cecil Rhodes, saw the possibilities of a new land and desired not to plunder it for gain, but to establish their own way of life and develop it for the benefit of their own countrymen and of the native races whose home it was.

A missionary spirit towards French Canada rose up in France in the reign of Louis XIII. Richelieu and his niece, Madame D'Aiguillon, sent to Quebec six workmen to clear the ground for a hospital, and founded the Hôtel-Dieu. The Cardinal supported with generosity the Jesuit mission to the Hurons. There is no finer story than that of the adventures of the Jesuits who went out to face not only dangers of climate, but death at the hands of the Indians, preceded by the most ingenious tortures that the Indian mind could devise. They literally went through fire and water in their martyrdom, and anyone who wishes to restore their faith in the heights to which human nature can rise, should read of their adventures in the lively pages of Francis Parkman. Those who survived helped in the work of colonisation, and those who died untimely have left an enduring mark on the history of Canada.

The devotion of the Jesuits is in marked contrast to the intrigue and double dealing at home, which prevented France's effort first to grasp and then to keep a hold on Canada. Francis I, Henry IV, Richelieu, and Louis XIV all dreamed of a Canadian Empire. But their hold on Canada was slender, partly owing to the disinclination of Frenchmen to leave the soil of their beloved France in any great numbers. It is an interesting historical fact that the French never gained a strong hold on New France until after the English conquest in 1759. The wisdom of their conquerors in giving them the right to practise their own Catholic faith and have their own separate schools helped the French to settle down and enjoy their new land, and to have such large families that they solved the problem of how to acquire a French population.

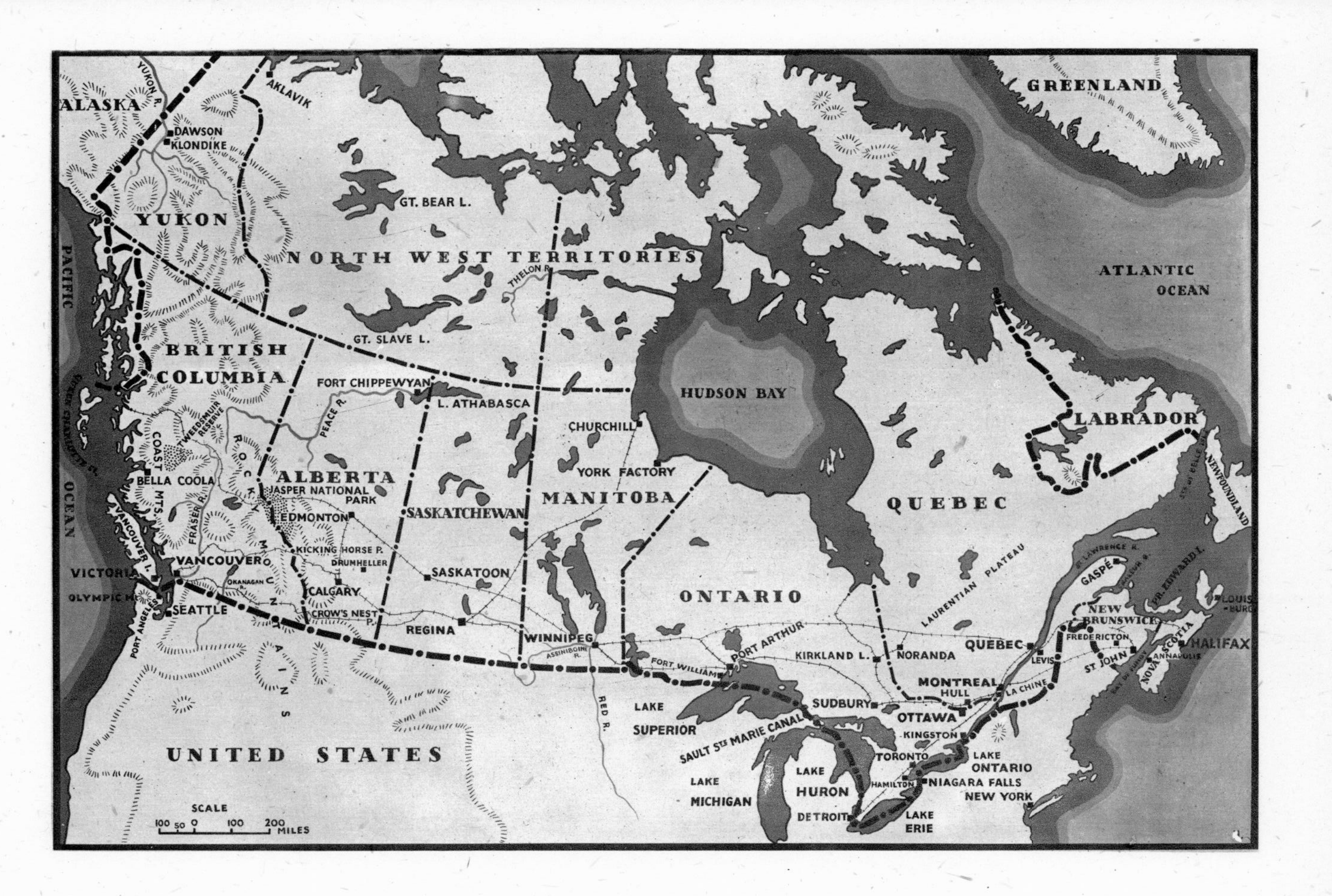
ALASKA
YUKON R.
DAWSON
KLONDIKE
AKLAVIK
YUKON
GT. BEAR L.
NORTH WEST TERRITORIES
THELON R.
GT. SLAVE L.
BRITISH COLUMBIA
FORT CHIPPEWYAN
L. ATHABASCA
PEACE R.
HUDSON BAY
CHURCHILL
YORK FACTORY
GREENLAND
ATLANTIC OCEAN
LABRADOR
NEWFOUNDLAND
PACIFIC OCEAN
COAST MTS.
TWEEDSMUIR RESERVE
BELLA COOLA
FRASER R.
ROCKY MOUNTAINS
ALBERTA
JASPER NATIONAL PARK
EDMONTON
KICKING HORSE P.
DRUMHELLER
CALGARY
CROW'S NEST P.
OKANAGAN
VANCOUVER I.
VANCOUVER
VICTORIA
OLYMPIC M.
SEATTLE
PORT ANGELES
SASKATCHEWAN
SASKATOON
REGINA
MANITOBA
WINNIPEG
ASSINIBOINE R.
RED R.
QUEBEC
LAURENTIAN PLATEAU
ONTARIO
PORT ARTHUR
FORT WILLIAM
KIRKLAND L.
NORANDA
QUEBEC
LEVIS
MONTREAL
HULL
LA CHINE
OTTAWA
SUDBURY
KINGSTON
TORONTO
HAMILTON
NIAGARA FALLS
NEW YORK
LAKE ONTARIO
LAKE ERIE
DETROIT
LAKE HURON
LAKE MICHIGAN
LAKE SUPERIOR
SAULT STE MARIE CANAL
GASPÉ
ST LAWRENCE R.
NEW BRUNSWICK
FREDERICTON
ST JOHN
NOVA SCOTIA
ANNAPOLIS
HALIFAX
LOUISBURG
PR. EDWARD I.
UNITED STATES
SCALE
100 50 0 100 200 MILES

MARQUIS DE MONTCALM
After a contemporary engraving

After Champlain, the Comte de Frontenac governed in Quebec. He was a soldier who had a small but brilliant court, with a states-general of clergy, nobility, and the third estate, on the French pattern. He conducted a feud with Bishop Laval over the burning question of selling liquor to the Indians—Frontenac was for control, Laval for prohibition. Laval was the wiser of the two men, for he foresaw the ruin that the potent *eau de vie*, to which the Indians took with such enthusiasm, might lead to. Frontenac's court was on the European model. He insisted on all the pomp of a governor-general, and it must have been a charming oasis of civilisation on the tall rock of Quebec, with the handsome clothes and refined civilisation of Louis XIV, set among savages and the wild desolation of the huge land, of which France held so little.

The student of Canadian history would do well to study the different types of colonisation of England and France in North America. The English colonies were better supported financially by the merchants of England than the French colonies by those of France. The struggle between England and France went on by land as well as by sea, both sides allying themselves with the Indians, and fighting fierce frontier warfare in deep snow, with the glare of burning villages in the sky.

But the fate of Canada largely hung on European happenings, and large pieces of it were ceded and re-ceded in different treaties by England and France to each other. The succeeding French governments were parochial in their outlook, attempting to govern Canadian possessions like a province of France, shackling the initiative of settlers by petty restrictions and feudal obligations. No doubt if England had had no interest in Canada, and the two countries had never clashed on the St. Lawrence, this would have righted itself in time, and the humbler settlers in Canada would have gained their self-government as the years passed. But this was not to be.

In 1749 the British founded Halifax and began to colonise Nova Scotia. In 1756 the Seven Years War started, and sea power finally decided the fate of Canada. The elder Pitt, Earl of Chatham, sent an expedition under a young

By courtesy of the Parker Gallery, London

INTERIOR OF FORT GARRY C. 1850: WINNIPEG MANITOBA

Chromograph by H. A. Strong

By courtesy of Leggatt Bros., London

A VIEW OF MONTREAL, 1850

Oil painting on papier maché produced by Jennens & Bettridge

commander, James Wolfe, in 1759. John Fortescue once said, " Curious face Wolfe's, profile like the flap of an envelope, long imperious nose and no chin at all." But in spite of his chinlessness Wolfe had commanding abilities and a wide experience of campaigning. The Marquis de Montcalm, his equal in high courage and integrity, with a fine military reputation behind him, commanded the French forces, on the tall rocks of Quebec. This position appeared to be impregnable, but Wolfe suspected a weak spot in the defences and sent part of his forces up a hidden and unguarded track. The capture of Quebec cost both of the armies their commander. Wolfe fell in the fighting on the summit of the rock, and Montcalm died of his wounds. Some say he was taken to the Ursuline Convent, and some to a house in St. Louis Street to die.

JAMES WOLFE
Engraved by R. Hanshaw, 1849, after the contemporary drawing by Captain Harvey Smith

As Wolfe was rowed across the St. Lawrence under cover of darkness he is said to have recited Gray's *Elegy*, pausing for a moment after repeating the line, " The paths of glory lead but to the grave." In his case this was a false prophecy. His path of glory led to an immortal fame, and his victory decided the fate of Canada. I have often looked at his memorial, round which Canadian children, French and English, play in Battlefields Park at Quebec, and read and re-read the inscription, " Here died Wolfe victorious," and thought of how few people such words could be remotely true.

Peace was made in 1763, and Canada was governed under a Royal Proclamation from England. A large slice of the continent, which France had dreamed of extending as far as the Mississippi and south to the Ohio, was arbitrarily joined with the province of Quebec. The British Government gave the Roman Catholic Church every privilege that had been enjoyed by that church, and French civil law and English commercial law flourished side by side.

In 1775 the American colonists, tired of George III's effort to impose laws and financial restrictions upon them, revolted. They invaded Canada, counting upon the help of the French Canadians. Montreal was captured and Quebec stood another siege during the winter of 1775-1776. But Sir Guy Carleton, afterwards Lord Dorchester, saved Quebec. The revolutionary army withdrew and Canada became the refuge and home of nearly forty thousand British loyalists, who were Tories unable to agree with the Whigs who had made the American Revolution and shaken off the rule of the Mother country. These colonists, settled in Nova Scotia, Ontario and New Brunswick, played a great part in the building of Canada. They were people of a resolute breed who gave up their homes and businesses to settle under the British flag. They and their descendants were characterised by a dignity and tenacity of character and keen intelligence. To belong to a U.E.L. (United Empire Loyalist) family is still to-day a considerable distinction, and U.E.L.'s are found in responsible positions all through the Dominion. The newly founded American nation refused to compensate them for their financial losses, but England recognised their claims and spent £400,000 in helping them.

After the victory of 1759 the Quebec Act of 1774 was the next event of paramount importance in the history of Canada, as it enabled the Roman Catholic faith and the French mode of life to flourish, and the descendants of the first French settlers to keep their own customs and culture under the ægis of British rule. Many difficulties were bound to arise later between the French and English, but French Canada has never forgotten that her interests lie with the country who

The Curfew tolls the Knell of parting Day,
The lowing Herd wind slowly o'er the Lea;
The Ploughman homeward plods his weary Way,
And leaves the World to Darkness & to me.
Now fades the glimm'ring Landscape on the Sight,
And all the Air a solemn Stillness holds;
Save where the Beetle wheels his droning Flight,
Or drowsy Tinklings lull the distant Folds.
Save that from yonder ivy-mantled Tower
The moping Owl does to the Moon complain
Of such, as wand'ring near her secret Bower
Molest her ancient solitary Reign.
Beneath those rugged Elms, that Yewtree's Shade,
Where heaves the Turf in many a mould'ring Heap,
Each in his narrow Cell for ever laid,
The rude Forefathers of the Hamlet sleep.
The breezy Call of incense-breathing Morn,
The Swallow twitt'ring from the straw-built Shed,
The Cock's shrill Clarion, & the ecchoing Horn,
No more shall rouse them from their lowly Bed.
For them no more the blazing Hearth shall burn,
Or busy Huswife ply her Evening Care;
No Children run to lisp their Sire's Return,
Nor climb his Knees the envied Kiss to share.
Oft did the Harvest to their Sickles yield,
Their Furrow oft the stubborn Glebe has broke;
How jocund did they drive their Team a-field!
How bow'd the Woods beneath their sturdy Stroke!
Let not Ambition mock their useful Toil,
Their homely Joys & Destiny obscure;
Nor Grandeur hear with a disdainful Smile
The short & simple Annals of the Poor.
The Boast of Heraldry, the Pomp of Power,
And all that Beauty, all that Wealth e'er gave,
Awaits alike th' inevitable Hour.
The Paths of Glory lead but to the Grave.
Forgive, ye Proud, th' involuntary Fault,
If Memory to These no Trophies raise,
Where thro' the long-drawn Ile & fretted Vault
The pealing Anthem swells the Note of Praise.
Can storied Urn or animated Bust
Back to its Mansion call the fleeting Breath?
Can Honour's Voice provoke the silent Dust,
Or Flatt'ry sooth the dull cold Ear of Death?

SOME VERSES OF GRAY'S "ELEGY" QUOTED BY GENERAL WOLFE
Facsimile extract from an original fair copy enclosed in a letter to Thomas Wharton, dated Cambridge, December 18th, 1750

TOWN AND HARBOUR OF HALIFAX NOVA SCOTIA
Drawn and engraved by R. Short 1769

allowed them to worship as they pleased, and which interfered in the hour of conquest neither with their religion nor their language.

Sir Guy Carleton distinguished himself not only in defending Quebec, but in the handling of the situation afterwards. Had he made the false step of treating the French-Canadians in the spirit of a conqueror there would have been dispeace in Canada and an endless legacy of bitterness. The Quebec Act is important as it showed a civilised toleration for the rights of a conquered minority ; also that England had not forgotten the lesson taught her by the Romans—freedom of custom under the law of the conqueror. In the eighteenth century this was by no means the usual procedure for a victorious nation.

The United States of America, as we must now call them, aimed at acquiring new territory, and purchased Louisiana for the price of a few million dollars. To conquer the thinly populated territories of Canada seemed an easy task, as Britain had her hands full trying to defend herself from Napoleon. Considerable resentment was caused on questions relating to shipping. British sailors who had been forcibly seized by press gangs in the coast towns of the British Isles gladly deserted at American ports, where people talked their own language and were kindly disposed towards them. British warships waiting near the port of New York stopped every vessel and removed from them to Halifax all the men who could be supposed to speak with an English, Scotch or Irish accent. The British Government forbade American, or any other neutral shipping from entering those parts of Europe under Napoleon's domination. Aggravated by these annoyances the United States Government planned a victorious march to Quebec, and in the year 1812 Congress declared war. The second great soldier of British stock in Canada's history was Isaac Brock, who, like Wolfe and Montcalm, had seen service on the continent of Europe. The war brought successes to both sides. General Brock took Detroit and fell at the battle of Queenston Heights in the hour of victory. The United States commander, General Petre, captured the little capital of York in Ontario (now Toronto), his soldiers returning after burning the Parliament house together with the Speaker's wig, which they exhibited as a human scalp to show how barbarous their opponents had been.

Britain's supremacy on the sea enabled her to harry the Atlantic coast of America. British soldiers took Washington and burned all the public buildings. It is said that before they set fire to the Presidential mansion, a regiment of Scottish soldiers devoured the dinner prepared for the President. Then they burnt as much of the house as they could, leaving only an outside shell. It is now called the White House for the reason that it was covered with white paint to conceal the marks of the burning.

The Treaty of Ghent settled this inconclusive war, which was a war of Governments and not of the peoples concerned. No concessions were made to either side, and frontiers remained unchanged. This little war holds much of interest to the military historian, but there are very few people in Britain, Canada or the United States who remember why it was fought or could name any of its battles.

Canada was divided into two provinces, Upper and Lower Canada (Ontario and Quebec), and while the French in Quebec strove to secure as much political power as possible for French Canadians, Ontario, which was predominantly British, struggled for democratic government of the people. England sent out governors to both provinces, usually Waterloo veterans who were more bluff than diplomatic, and who in Lower Canada succeeded each other with bewildering frequency.

Two revolts typical of the attitude of mind of Upper and Lower Canada took place in 1837. Joseph Papineau, the owner of a seigneury on the St. Lawrence, and a fiery politician, started a rebellion which had for its object a French republic on the St. Lawrence. William Lyon Mackenzie, an ancestor of the present Prime Minister of Canada, also took up arms against the government of the Ontario province, which was ruled by an official class who were closely related to each other by intermarriage. Neither revolt succeeded. Lord Durham, who was sent out from England, was recalled after five months, but the Durham Report (1839) laid the foundations of a policy which has endured. He recommended the union of Upper and Lower Canada, and the granting to all British North America a measure of full self-government. The two provinces were each given a separate Parliament. It was a long time before the union of the two provinces worked in any kind of harmony. In 1867 the British North America Act was drawn up, and the Dominion of Canada came into existence. It included Ontario, Quebec, New Brunswick and Nova Scotia.

PLAIN CREES DRIVING BUFFALOES INTO A POUND
Engraving from " Hind's Exploring Expeditions 1857 and 1858 "

The history of Canada began by being the history of the Maritime provinces, Quebec and parts of Ontario. The conquest of the West was yet to come. While the wife of the Governor of Lower Canada recorded in her diary in the middle 1830's the comfort of her room in the Château St. Louis at Quebec, with hothouse roses and mignonette on her table in the winter, and her pleasant round of social activities, the Indians in the West at that time had seldom seen a white man, and herds of buffalo and caribou grazed untroubled by human interference, and the great forests slumbered in unbroken silence.

But as long ago as 1670 Charles II had granted a charter to his cousin Prince Rupert and seventeen other noblemen and gentlemen, amongst whom was the great Duke of Marlborough, to trade with the Indians for furs. This small company took the name of " The Governor and Company of Adventurers Trading into Hudson Bay." This was a very important step, as the Hudson's Bay Company has been responsible, in some part, for the building up and development of Canada. At first it traded for furs with the Indians in all lands watered by streams flowing into Hudson Bay. It encountered strong rivalry from other fur traders, and after many years of strife amalgamated with the North-west Fur Company of Montreal in 1821. The Hudson's Bay Company have always been pioneers and have made homes in remote places all over the northern part of the continent, and opened up the country far more quickly than any government could have done. It was an instance of the flag following trade, not the reverse as is usually the case.

In 1789 a fur trader, Alexander Mackenzie, determined to explore as far as the Pacific. He left Fort Chippewyan on Lake Athabasca, travelling to Great Slave Lake, and thence to a mighty river at the west end of the lake, believing that this would take him to the Pacific. He was much disappointed to find himself in the Arctic. In May of the next year he made his epic journey to the Pacific. His guides were sullen and mutinous (also verminous, as he noticed when he camped near them at night). They crossed great lakes and mountains and rivers, the whole expedition held together by Mackenzie's own resolve to push on. At last, after crossing a range of mountains, they reached Bella Coola on the Pacific coast. The friendly Bella Coola Indians feasted the expedition on salmon and lent them a canoe. On a rock which still stands, Mackenzie painted the inscription, "Alexander Mackenzie from Canada by land, the twenty-second of July, one thousand seven hundred and ninety-three." Canada has fortunately never lacked men of tenacious courage who would traverse vast distances to conquer her geographical secrets.

The uniting of the whole of Canada into a Dominion came slowly with some harsh and painful episodes. The first white settlement in Manitoba was made by Pierre Gaultier de Varennes, Sieur de la Verandrye, who died in 1749. In 1738 he built Fort Rouge at the junction of the Red and the Assiniboine rivers.

In 1811 a Scotsman, the Earl of Selkirk, brought out settlers from the Highlands. He purchased land from the Hudson's Bay Company and landed a number of crofters at York Factory, Hudson Bay. In August, 1812, they reached the fort from which was to grow the city of Winnipeg. This scheme failed, and Lord Selkirk was compelled to bring in soldiers to quell a threatened massacre of the new settlers. He died in the south of France in 1820, shattered in health and a saddened and disappointed man. But he had started the settlement of western Canada, which was to become one of the largest granaries of the world.

Lord Selkirk's scheme had greatly increased the population. For a time the settlers lived quietly under the rule of the Hudson's Bay Company. In 1869 the newly formed Dominion of Canada bought territory from the Company and began to send in officials to survey roads and lay out the framework of the new towns. The original settlers of Manitoba, Scotch and French farmers, had inter-married with the Indians, and their half-breed descendants were named the Metis. They farmed, fished, and trapped for furs, and desired no interference from outside. They disliked the idea of new towns being laid out, and foresaw the decimation of the wild animal life of the province if there was a new influx of population. Louis Riel, a half-breed, led an unsuccessful rebellion of the Metis, which had to be quelled by an expedition under Sir Garnet Wolseley.

Provision had been made by the British North America Act to receive new provinces into the Dominion. Manitoba was the first to come in. In 1871 British Columbia also entered the fold, on the promise that there should be a railway constructed which would connect that province with the eastern part of the Dominion. In 1878 an Imperial Order in Council was passed annexing to the Dominion all British possessions in North America (except Newfoundland). The Canadian Pacific Railway was completed in 1885, the last spike being driven in by Mr. Donald Smith (afterwards Lord Strathcona), whose fortune had been largely pledged to this undertaking.

THE CANADIAN PACIFIC RAILWAY
Kicking Horse Canyon, British Columbia

The building of the railway was an epic of danger and difficulty : its constructors had to contend with flood and fire, the hostility of the Indians, and the appalling engineering problems which would in themselves have been hard enough to surmount. Canada could not build the line with her own resources, it was said, and the critics decided that the undertaking was hopeless. More than once the project faced bankruptcy. The tenacity of Van Horne, a railway constructor from the United States, carried the day, and at a very dark moment, when the money for the enterprise had almost run out, Van Horne convinced the Prime Minister, Sir John Macdonald, that the ruining of the company which was building the railway would be also the ruin of Canada. The Banks in London believed in the project and provided the capital for the railway, so that the million promised by Canada was never paid up. The railway was a miracle of engineering. Sometimes the lines were laid at the rate of three miles a day on the prairies. The Kicking Horse Pass was chosen as the way through the Rocky Mountains, where the railway has to climb five thousand feet to get through the pass. It reached the Pacific up the mouth of the Fraser River, where now stands the important city of Vancouver.

After the completion of the railway steamships began to ply across the Great Lakes and along the shores of the Pacific. Emigrants flowed into the prairies and the whole life of Canada could circulate freely between east and west.

The opening years of the twentieth century saw more railways built, the railway systems of the Canadian Northern and the Grand Trunk being added to that of the Canadian Pacific, which helped to create a general fusion of the whole Dominion from coast to coast. King Wheat and King Gold, those potent factors for wealth above and below the ground, brought more emigrants, who made settlements, with churches and schools. Huge deposits of nickel were found at Sudbury, gold deposits in the waters of the Yukon, coal deposits near the Crow's Nest Pass, gold and copper at Noranda and Kirkland Lake, and later pitchblende deposits at Great Bear Lake, to mention in passing a few of the most famous names in mining. The forests began to provide a wealth of wood pulp suitable for newsprint, which was exported to both the United States and to England. To the lover of beauty it seems painfully sad to sacrifice acres of forest daily to produce the issues of the yellow press, but on the wood pulp exports much of Canada's present wealth and prosperity is based.

The Dominion has seen some great Prime Ministers. Sir John A. Macdonald served his country in public life for over forty years, and laid down the foundation of the policy for making Canada a confederated state within the Empire. Sir Wilfrid Laurier, a French Canadian, became Prime Minister in 1896. During his administration Canada became increasingly prosperous. A stream of emigrants arrived from both Europe and the United States. In 1905 two new provinces were formed out of the District of the North-West Territories, and Alberta and Saskatchewan came into being. Canada sent a contingent of troops to the South African war in 1899, which included the famous Strathcona Horse, raised and equipped by Lord Strathcona, High Commissioner for the Dominion in London.

By courtesy of the British Museum

ESQUIMAUX ATTACKING AN ENGLISH BOAT FROM THEIR CAYAKS
Water colour drawing attributed to John White

By courtesy of the Parker Gallery, London

A PICNIC TO MONTMORENCI

From a set of six coloured lithographs by A. Krieghoff

To write of the history near one's own time is always more difficult than to dig into a remoter past. It is easier to describe the adventurers and administrators who have all the glamour of picturesque clothes and environment than to describe their successors in frock coats who made treaties about tariffs.

But in 1914 Canada embarked on another great adventure, when she fought for the second time at the side of Britain. Canadians left their farms, their trapping and fishing, and their businesses, large and small, coming across the ocean as fast as ships could bring them. In the air, on sea, and on land, they won an immortality of fame as fighters. The battles of Second Ypres, when they sustained the first gas attack of the war ; of Valenciennes and above all of Vimy Ridge, showed their magnificent fighting quality. The German respect for the Canadians as fighters was seen in captured maps, which indicated the great number of German divisions always maintained opposite the trenches where the Canadians were known to be.

Canada has now come for the third time to help Britain, and when the battle is joined the sons of the men who fought at Ypres and Vimy will show that they are made of the same fighting stuff as their fathers.

In 1926 the Imperial Conference met in London, a century and a half after the angry colonists in America had met in Philadelphia in a mood of flaming resentment to define their relationship with Great Britain. The Imperial Conference laid down that Britain herself and the self-governing communities of the Empire " are equal in status and in no way subordinate to one another in any respect of their domestic or external affairs (though united by a common allegiance to the Crown) and freely associated as members of the British Commonwealth of Nations."

Thus, George V, descendant of George III (who had lost us our American colonies), became the link which held the Empire of 1926 together. Five years later the British Parliament passed the Statute of Westminster, renouncing its authority over Canada and the other self-governing states of the Empire, which thus became completely sovereign nations.

These brief words about Canada's history will perhaps serve to show how Canada has grown up from the wilderness, in which man held a precarious foothold, to a sovereign power. Although she has several times been invaded by her blood relations south of the border she cherishes none of the dark and tragic resentments which we see in Europe, and lives beside her neighbour, the United States, in the greatest friendliness. As I write, in September, 1940, Canada and America have established a joint Defence Board which meets in Ottawa.

A VIEW OF LOUISBOURG IN 1758 WHEN THE CITY WAS BESEIGED
Contemporary line engraving printed for Carington Bowles

II.

A BIRD'S EYE VIEW OF THE PROVINCES.

THE Maritime Provinces have the charm held by all sea coast countries. In Nova Scotia you are never more than thirty miles from the sound of the sea. The apple trees, laden down with fruit, in the Annapolis valley are seen silhouetted against blue water. You eat excellent fish, and large and splendid lobsters appear on every table. The soft landscape and the villages, each grouped round its church, suggest an England transplanted somehow into a clearer air.

The people of Nova Scotia are mainly of English and Scottish descent. The province abounds in coal which, with fishing and apple growing, makes for prosperity. Halifax was founded two hundred years ago, and her Parliament House has portraits of the Georges, delightful mantelpieces, and an old library. Halifax has one of the largest and most important harbours in the British Empire ; long and narrow, it offers a particularly safe anchorage for ships.

During the Seven Years war that ended in the conquest of Canada by Britain, the government took the harsh step of deporting the French citizens from the district called Acadia, who, although they had been under British rule since 1713, had still kept their allegiance to France.

VIEW OF THE FALLS OF CHAUDIÈRE YUKON
Aquatint by J. W. Edy after G. B. Fisher

In 1758 the Fort of Louisbourg was captured by the English and destroyed. It had been France's strongest fortress in North America. It had been so extremely costly to build, that a King of France had once enquired if the streets were indeed paved with gold. The ghost of the Evangeline of Longfellow's poem still haunts the countryside, and many tourists who would never dream of ploughing their way through this lengthy epic, gaze respectfully at her statue and take away picture postcards of her garden as souvenirs.

St. John in New Brunswick stands on the Bay of Fundy, a place dreaded by captains of ships because of the fogs which are apt to lurk there and make navigation difficult. It began as a settlement of United Empire Loyalists. The capital of the province of New Brunswick is Fredericton, which has a late 18th century charm about it. It has government buildings and a small cathedral. The province lies between the American border on the south and the province of Quebec on the north. The interior of New Brunswick is wooded, and paper mills turn the forest trees into pulp.

The third of the Maritime Provinces is Prince Edward Island. In a country as vast as Canada it is pleasant to find an island province of two thousand square miles with a population of ninety thousand people, chiefly engaged in mixed farming; with a Lieutenant-Governor living in a charming house, and a Parliament House which carries on the business of the province on the model of the Parliament in London. It has one of the biggest farms in the world for breeding foxes for their pelts. The soil of the island is red, like that of Devonshire.

The Maritimers are a hard-working and hard-headed people who are found in positions of trust and responsibility all through the Dominion.

The traveller who sails up the St. Lawrence river is struck by the way strips of cultivation run down to the edge of the water, and by the size of the churches compared to the smallness of the villages. While the other denominations in Canada are mostly content to imitate the Gothic when they build a church, the French Canadian churches have an individuality all their own. Their slim silvery spires reflect the sunshine in the winter, and they stand out like jewels against the snow.

Canada is emphatically the land of contrasts, and the traveller who arrives at Quebec may see old-fashioned horse-drawn buggies alongside the most modern and stream-lined cars. Tourists are fond of sitting perched up in these buggies, which are to be seen making a rather perilous way up and down the steep streets of Quebec.

The first impression you receive if you arrive at Quebec railway station is that you have strayed into a square in a French town. Then your car takes an almost perpendicular tilt, and you are borne rapidly up the hill to the central square, from which you see the mountains and the wide St. Lawrence.

Sightseers find a great deal to interest them in Quebec. There is the Ursuline Convent, the Hôtel Dieu, founded in 1639 by Cardinal Richelieu's niece, the Duchess d'Aiguillon. Here are also many other points of interest. Quebec attracts thousands of American tourists. Except for New Orleans it is the only city in North America where modernity and age go side by side.

The Governor-General's official residence, the Citadel, stands on the top of the cliffs. It has all the charm of a fortress and the amenities of a country house. It stands in the barrack square, where a regimental band plays, and La Royale 22ième Régiment (who have recently been on guard at Buckingham Palace) salute and present arms, and the sentries tramp up and down. The Governors of Lower Canada lived in the Château St. Louis. It was burnt down, and the Château Frontenac Hotel stands on its site. From the terrace at the Citadel you are dazzled by a vista of mountains and water ; opposite, across the St. Lawrence, are the houses of the town of Levis, and many church spires which catch the sunset light. Beyond them the foot-hills undulate to the mountains on the United States border. To the left you see the flagstaff, whence flies the Governor-General's flag (when he is in residence at the Citadel), and the waters of the St. Lawrence. They are spanned by a bridge between the mainland and the Island of Orleans. Upon that small and enchanting island you may see oxen ploughing, and women weaving in traditional patterns. In the villages and the churches you seem to have entered an older and more peaceful world.

Quebec is a French city with a small English population. Montreal is the third largest French town in the world. From the Mountain, the public park at Montreal which surmounts the city, you can see magnificent views and listen to the hum of the streets, and see the spires of churches and a convent, and the ships in the thronged and busy port.

Life in the country in French Canada is integrated, homely and hard-working. The " habitants " speak a French which descends from the seven-

By courtesy of the Parker Gallery, London

VIEW OF SAINT JOHN, NEW BRUNSWICK, 1851
Coloured lithograph after J. W. Hill by N. Sarony

By courtesy of the Author

WINTER IN THE GATINEAU : QUEBEC PROVINCE
Crayon by Frank Hennessey

THE CITADEL OF QUEBEC
Engraving by Challis after Bartlett from " Canadian Scenery " published 1842

teenth century, and have enormous families, traditional to that epoch. There were approximately 60,000 French inhabitants in 1763 when Canada became British. Now the French population has grown to over three million, and it is sometimes said that in another fifty years (unless the population of English-speaking Canada grows by immigration) it will be outnumbered easily by the French Canadians.

In spite of the influence of the Roman Catholic Church, whose policy is to promote contentment with rural life, there has been a tendency for the country people to flock into Montreal and other towns, and for the young men to seek work in the New England mills. But French Canadians make good farmers, clearing and working the roughest and stoniest of soils. They have produced more lawyers, doctors, politicians, artisans and craftsmen than men of business. Nearly all big business in Montreal is in the hands of English-speaking Canadians.

The province of Quebec has spectacular beauty of scenery, and endless possibilities for the hunter and fisherman. Some of it is still unexplored, and a great deal of it completely unknown. It produces many valuable furs, and much lumber and pulp for paper. This French province, with so many historic traditions, and so much care for its language and devotion to its ancient culture has an especial charm. French Canadians love bright colours. Lumbermen wear vivid blue and scarlet jerseys when at work. Rugs woven in the province are gay in design, and have a real quality of their own, so have the little carved

AERIAL VIEW OF OTTAWA
Showing the Dominion Houses of Parliament and Château Laurier

and painted figures of monks, nuns, habitants and their wives. But in spite of her love of the French language French Canada cares very little for France. She belongs neither quite to the Old nor to the New World, but is unique and incalculable and altogether charming.

Ottawa, the capital of Canada, is in Ontario on the Ottawa river. It lies near the Gatineau hills, with their lakes and forests. These stretch away to the wilder woods of the north. The Parliament Buildings stand on a bluff overlooking the river and the French city of Hull on the opposite side.

Parliament and the Senate meet in Ottawa, and the Governor-General has his official residence on the outskirts of the city, where he is guarded by Royal Canadian Mounted Police. Rideau Hall is surrounded by a charming park in which black squirrels and chipmunks play hide and seek in the grass. Since 1926 the Governor-General no longer represents the British Government in Canada. He is chosen by Canada in consultation with the reigning King of England, and is purely the King's representative. He opens Parliament preceded by a mounted escort and hailed by a salute of guns ; holds with his wife a drawing-room every year in the Senate Chamber ; travels in his private cars on the Dominion railways, and is the channel by which all communications from the Dominion go to Buckingham Palace.

NIAGARA FALLS
Part of the Canadian Falls

THE FISH MARKET TORONTO ONTARIO *c.* 1850
Oil painting on papier maché produced by Jennens & Bettridge

The British High Commissioner, whose functions are the same as those of the Canadian High Commissioner in London, has also an official house in Ottawa, and the diplomatic corps all have their headquarters in the city. The population of Ottawa is composed largely of civil servants, and in the parliamentary season it is thronged by members of Parliament and Senators from all parts of Canada. During the winter life in Ottawa is gay and sociable. In the summer many people go away to camps or cottages by the lakes and in the hills.

Ottawa has a picture gallery containing an admirable collection of old masters, as well as modern Canadian and other pictures ; also an excellent museum, and an archives building for students of Canadian history.

Dwellers in Ottawa can soon reach completely rural solitudes, and in the winter the whole sunny landscape is alive with skiers, dressed in brilliant colours. In the fall people walk and drive through the woods in the Gatineau valley, admiring the peach and cornelian coloured leaves on the trees, contrasted with the purple of the hills and the sapphire blue of the lakes.

About sixty per cent. of the population of the province of Ontario is urban. It contains one-third of the population, and more than half the wealth of Canada. The St. Lawrence forms the frontier there with the United States. The northern boundary of the province is on Hudson Bay. The falls of Niagara, vast, noisy and imposing, draw every year crowds of sightseers, while the Niagara peninsula is a paradise for fruit growers. Farming in Ontario is very productive and is of a very high and scientific quality, and the farms have something of the settled and peaceful appearance of farms in England.

There are great forests in Northern Ontario. In the winter the train passes through unending aisles of what appear to be Christmas trees, their roots deep

KINGSTON ONTARIO *c.* 1850
Oil painting on papier maché produced by Jennens & Bettridge

in snow. In summer you see the vivid green of the treacherous muskegs, an occasional wooden shack, with a flutter of washing on a line, varying the monotony. But in this curiously savage country many valuable minerals have been found, and the mining development of Northern Ontario has surprised the world. Prospecting for new mines goes on all the time.

In contrast to the lonely remoteness of the northern parts we find in Toronto a large city with a great university, sophisticated shops and fine public buildings. The outward aspect of Toronto is American, but it is deeply British in sentiment. Kingston, Hamilton, and many other towns in Ontario have a pleasant long-settled air about them, and there are many villages with leafy avenues of trees, whose golden leaves in the fall contrast pleasantly with the red brick of the houses.

The vast bodies of fresh water, Lakes Superior and Huron, two of the chain of five known as the Great Lakes, lie between Ontario and the United States. Their season of navigation, which is controlled by the opening and closing of the Sault Ste. Marie Canal, is about eight months in length. Through Port Arthur and Fort William, two ports which lie a short distance apart, the grain from the prairies is shipped eastwards. They are pleasant towns with impressive grain elevators which become packed with wheat to bursting point after a good harvest.

There are no tides in the Great Lakes, but spring and autumn gales can raise dangerous seas on their otherwise peaceful surface. These great inland lakes give an even greater feeling of immensity than the sea, as the eye travels over their clear, calm waters stretching apparently into infinity.

From Ontario we reach the Prairie Provinces. Winnipeg stands in the centre of the North American continent on the wheat belt. It has huge Parlia-

REAPERS CUTTING GRAIN ON A FARM
Alberta

ment buildings and is the headquarters of the Hudson's Bay Company. Its prosperity advances and recedes with the prosperity of the wheat growers on the prairie. A visit to the Grain Exchange is puzzling to the uninitiated. Apparently angry men mutter and shout in what appears to be an unknown language ; but that is the way in which wheat has been bought and sold ever since Winnipeg was a city.

Some people find the prairies monotonous, but those who enjoy looking over wide spaces under a huge expanse of sky will find their endless undulations very satisfying, whether in winter when they are deep in snow, or just before the harvest when the tall ears of wheat ripple and bend in the wind as far as the eye can see. The prairie people rarely want to leave for other places in Canada. Everywhere else seems to them rather confined and cramping after the huge expanses to which they are accustomed. The price of wheat is the determining factor in prosperity or privation on the prairies. The farmers and their wives often spend lives of incessant toil. A drought, hail, and grass-hoppers spell tragedy and disaster. But they are a virile people who get a great deal of pleasure out of life even in hard times, and some of the ablest Canadian minds have come from the prairies.

Life in the prairie provinces in summer is built around the absorbing drama of the growth and harvesting of the wheat crop. The prairie farmer, and all

WHEAT ELEVATORS AT PORT ARTHUR ON LAKE SUPERIOR
Ontario

who work to produce his implements and means of production, labour day and night from early spring until the dramatic days in August, when, if sun and rain have been kind, the crop is cut, bound and threshed. If the crop or the price has failed he must look forward to a long winter, thrown back on his own resources for entertainment. If the crop is successful the farmer may reckon to take his family south or west to a sunnier clime for the winter.

In Western Alberta among the foothills of the Rockies, where the ranching land lies, life is more picturesque and less mechanised than in any other part of the Dominion. It is a land of big ranches where life is fast moving and gay in summer, and desperately arduous in winter.

The two cities of Saskatchewan, Regina and Saskatoon, are now large and important. So is Calgary in Alberta, which has grown in living memory from a few shacks to a modern town with a hundred thousand inhabitants. The Calgary Stampede which takes place yearly is a wonderful sight. People come to it from all over North America, and the shifting crowds of Indians and their squaws and babies, Mounties, farmers in faded coats and leather breeches, cowboys with " ten gallon " hats, and smartly dressed women, have great gaiety and charm. The Indians spend the whole year preparing for it, and the local tribe of Stoney Indians ride rangy prairie ponies which they have bred.

THE CALGARY STAMPEDE
Alberta

The cowboys perform amazing feats sitting bucking broncos, and conducting rodeo exhibitions.

Edmonton, north of Calgary, is a city which is growing rapidly. It is now regarded as the gateway of the north, through which the riches of oil, grain and minerals will come. In the North of Alberta is the Peace River country, which extends into British Columbia. It is often called the " country of beginning again " as so many people from the prairie drought areas and from distressed countries in Europe have settled there. The crops are magnificent and the flowers are huge in size and extraordinarily brilliant in colouring, owing to the long hours of sunshine in the summer.

Alberta has two national parks which are holiday playgrounds of wonderful beauty. Jasper is a paradise for those who like to observe wild life in circumstances of great comfort to themselves. Deer and bear wander fearlessly in the woods and upon the golf course. In hot weather the bears sometimes turn on the sprinklers on the greens in order to cool themselves. They are not dangerous if care is taken not to tease them, but they often raid larders in the camps and picnic baskets in cars. Above all they love the hotel ash heaps, where they can be seen in twos and threes scooping pineapple juice out of tins and devouring the remains of any other delicacies they can find.

From Jasper it is easy to go up and camp on one of the many lakes. For one whole afternoon on Beaver Lake I watched (while the rest of the party were catching many fish) two moose who had come down to the water's edge to devour lily roots. With their blunt and rudimentary set of horns and long ugly faces, they looked strangely like pantomime animals. Above our heads towered the peaks of the Rockies, their slanting tops showing dark against the sky.

So much has been written about the Rocky Mountains that it is unnecessary to add another tribute to their spectacular beauty and magnificence. As the train swings, winds, ascends and descends you see them at a multitude of angles, catching now a glimpse of a long valley with an emerald coloured lake, now

By courtesy of the Rt. Hon. R. B. Bennett

THE THREE SISTERS : NEAR BANFF ALBERTA
Oil painting by R. Gissing

By courtesy of the Rt. Hon. R. B. Bennett

CHINOOK IN THE FOOTHILLS : ALBERTA

THE BROWN BEAR
Banff National Park, Alberta

looking upward at the flank of some great peak. If you journey through the Rockies in the spring you may see snow almost level with the tops of the telegraph poles; great snow slopes painted all colours by the bright winter sunshine.

It is a charming surprise to wake up in Vancouver and see clumps of pussy willow in flower outside the windows of the train. Vancouver is a growing city and an extremely important port. Its partly oriental population makes it picturesque. Grave Sikhs with black turbans are to be seen walking in the streets, and stolid-faced Chinamen stand under cabalistic signs in front of their shops. The tall buildings have a spectacular backdrop of snow-covered mountains behind them. It is a very busy port and has a big trade with the Pacific seaboard of the United States and the Far East. All manner of craft are seen in the harbour, from luxury yachts and liners to the queer-shaped boats covered by a small awning, which the Japanese use for fishing.

You leave for Victoria in a comfortable Canadian Pacific boat, and go on a fairy voyage, almost touching a multitude of islands. Vancouver Island might be called "Little England of the Pacific." It has a climate much resembling that of the British Isles and is rarely very cold and never oppressively warm. Some of the inhabitants of Victoria who have retired from active life, walk about in ancient tweeds with dogs at their heels. Gardening is pursued with ardour and the beauty of the flowers grown on the island is great. Flower shows are very popular, and the fields of daffodils grown for marketing are a lovely sight.

The architecture of Victoria is pleasantly Victorian, with solid villas set in flowers and grass, and the only alien note is the Chinese gardener gravely watering precious seedlings. In spite of its sedate mode of life this island has still wild animals, and the Forbidden Plateau (so called because of Indian legend) is not yet completely explored. Except for a few logging camps the north end of the island is almost uninhabited.

BISON IN THE BANFF NATIONAL PARK
Alberta

One of the most famous features of Vancouver Island is its tall Douglas firs which throw all tree lovers into an ecstasy of delight. Their red trunks soar into the sky at a great height. The famous Cathedral Grove gives one an impression of immense dignity, and in the soft gloom under the trees you seem to be walking in a temple of the out-of-doors. The Malahat Drive shows you bays and islands succeeding each other at every turn of the road. A day in a yacht gives you a view of every kind of island, big or small. From Victoria you look across the straits towards Port Angeles and Seattle, and to the splendid Olympic mountains, whose peaks are crowned with ice fields which glitter like diamonds in the sun. This view changes continually and is one of the miracles of the world.

The Pacific coast presents a most curious contrast, for it is largely settled by the people who have come from England. In the most tropical and exotic of Canada's provinces one finds rooms where all the furniture has come from some English country house, and where English food and customs are reproduced exactly. To attempt to describe the amenities of British Columbia would be to embark on a eulogy more fitted to a travel agent's catalogue. In the vicinity of Vancouver one can ski, even in summer, by taking a perpendicular motor run of a few thousand feet, and descend in the same day to bathe in the

MOUNT EDITH CAVELL JASPER NATIONAL PARK
Alberta

VANCOUVER
British Columbia

Pacific. In Victoria one can play golf at Oak Bay with the ocean lapping the course on three sides, or sail a boat among the myriad islands of the gulf. Vancouver Island has a cosier and more intimate charm than much of the rest of Canada. Life moves at a slower tempo than elsewhere, and many people retire there to end their days in the enjoyment of its peace and beauty.

British Columbia was discovered in 1774 by a Spaniard named Perez. Captain Vancouver surveyed the whole coast of the province between 1792 and 1794; about the same time that Alexander Mackenzie entered it. For twenty-eight years the Hudson's Bay Company ruled this territory despotically but with benevolence. In 1849 Vancouver Island became a British colony, and in 1858, after the discovery of gold, there was a great influx of population on the mainland. In 1866 it united with Vancouver Island and became the colony of British Columbia.

In 1871 British Columbia entered the confederation and became part of the Dominion of Canada, sending Senators and Members of Parliament as representatives to the Parliament at Ottawa.

The Indian tribes in British Columbia have an interesting history and a distinctive art of their own. It runs to the grotesque in the tall totem poles and the curious symbolism upon carved chests and strips of needlework. But

CARVED HOUSE-POSTS AND TOTEM POLES OF THE HAIDA INDIANS
Queen Charlotte Islands

each part of the design has its own meaning and tells to the initiated a vivid story expressed in a few lines.

The province is very rich in fisheries. The Fraser river alone has yearly large runs of salmon which are taken to canneries where they are cut up and packed into tins and sent to England and to the United States. There is a steady demand for British Columbian lumber. The province also has a large variety of trees, spruce, cedar, Douglas firs, etc. There is good agricultural land, and mixed farming flourishes both in Vancouver Island and on the mainland. Much care is given to the raising of fruit, especially in the Okanagan Valley, where apples, plums and cherries are grown.

The Coast Range of mountains has great beauty and variety of scenery. From Bella Coola to Prince Rupert the steamer runs in and out of fiords which much resemble Norway. A great deal of this country was settled by Norwegians, and when one sits down to a Norwegian repast in a charmingly designed wooden house, it is difficult to realise that you are near the Pacific and not the North Sea.

British Columbia is bounded on the north partly by the Yukon Territories, made famous by the gold rush to the Klondike mines in 1896, when men grew rich overnight and Dawson City saw all the extremes of wealth and poverty.

THE HABITANT FARM
Water colour by C. Krieghoff

Unlike British Columbia, which has a maritime climate, the Yukon has a very severe winter, sometimes lasting for seven months, but with a brilliant and sunny summer.

The Northern Territories of Canada are vast in extent, stretching up into the Arctic circle. Most parts of them are unexplored, but Aklavik has a hospital, a church and a hotel, and various mines have settlements around them. Life can be made comfortable, and the radio has linked the North to the rest of the world. The development of the North is largely dependent upon the aeroplane, which can open up these Territories in a way undreamed of thirty years ago. Machinery is flown in by plane to some of the northern mines, and even cattle make this journey, in what must seem to them a strange proximity to the sky. Very sick people are flown from lonely places to hospitals where they can receive treatment. Canada already sends more freight by air mail than any country in the world.

Tribes of Eskimos live in the north from Greenland to Alaska. They are a merry people, squat in appearance with broad faces. They have an original native art of carving animal and human figures from walrus ivory, and the women embroider patterns in bead work on their clothes. Eskimos have also a flair for mechanics. There is a legend that an Eskimo was given a gold watch. He had never before seen such a thing, but he took it to pieces and reconstructed it correctly in the space of twenty-four hours. Diesel engines and other machinery soon are open books to the Eskimo. They live by trapping for furs

VIEW IN THE ARCTIC REGIONS
Water colour by Sir George Back, *c.* 1838

and killing whales and seals, and, largely owing to the far-sighted policy of the Hudson's Bay Company, are untouched by liquor traffic or the baser side of civilisation. They seldom wash, and wear fur and leather clothes. An Eskimo girl is eagerly sought in marriage if she is handy with her needle. They laugh a great deal, and think that people who get angry and fly into rages are insane and only fit to be put into holes in the ice. Eskimos are immensely hardy, going numberless miles by dog teams over ice and snow, sometimes in blizzards. At night they construct a house out of snow or blocks of ice.

The animals of the northern parts of the North-West Territories are mostly fur-bearing ; musk oxen are found on the Thelon Barrens and in Ellesmere Land, and great flocks of ducks, geese and other migrants spend summer in the northern wilds.

III.

THE CANADIAN WAY OF LIFE.

1

THE exact differences in the way of living of different nations is a hard matter to assess, for although they arise in the main from varying economic and geographical conditions there are also many subtler influences.

Canadians are proud of maintaining that they combine the best in the New and the Old Worlds ; that they have received what is vigorous and progressive in American thought and material improvement, whilst retaining all that is compatible in the dignified and stately heritage of their French and English past. To a very great extent this is true ; scientific improvement is more widely diffused than in England, and manners are more easily and unconstrainedly democratic. At the same time, in the universities, in the professions, and in public life, customs and methods are reminiscent of the less hurried and more dignified ways of their English counterparts.

The English and the American visitor to Canada feel that they are both coming home and visiting a foreign land. The Englishman recognises the Union Jack flying over all public buildings, the use of the same names for public and municipal offices, and he feels that common tie, allegiance to the Crown ; but in the material things he is astonished by the size of the trains, the extremes of climate, and the use of the words " sidewalk," " street-car " and " elevator " for " pavement," " tram " and " lift." While the American who crosses the border hears the same slang used in the streets, may see the same films as at home, the same kind of architecture and agriculture, but feels puzzled and a little lost in a country which visualises loyalty to the Crown of England as a prior duty to loyalty to its own duly elected government, and which runs its army, navy and the public services so like, but yet so unlike his own.

In a country so vast as Canada, where distances are hard to overcome, it is impossible to generalise about the way in which people work and enjoy themselves. In the towns of the Maritime Provinces life is lived at the quiet tempo usually associated with English cathedral towns of the last century ; while in summer some of the finest salmon rivers in the world and a coast perfect for all forms of sailing provide marvellous means of enjoyment. Montreal and Toronto have all the diversions of big cities coupled with vigorous university and intellectual life. While the country districts of Quebec have an atmosphere which is comparable to nothing either in England or the United States, country life in Ontario is very like life as it is lived on a big farm in England. What makes urban life in Eastern Canada unlike anything in England or Europe, except Switzerland, is that country pursuits are open to even the poorest inhabitants. The snowy slopes of the Laurentians in winter, and the endless chains of lakes which lie among them in summer, make ski-ing and skating, swimming and fishing really accessible to all.

By courtesy of the Author

THE SUGAR BUSH: QUEBEC PROVINCE

Crayon by Frank Hennessey

By courtesy of the Author

A BRITISH COLUMBIAN FOREST
Water colour by Emily Carr

CANADIAN MOUNTIE ON PATROL IN BANFF NATIONAL PARK
Alberta

2

The names of the R.C.M.P. (Royal Canadian Mounted Police) and the Hudson's Bay Company are familiar even to those who know nothing else about Canada. The former are a prominent feature in the life of the Dominion. They are careful guardians of law and order, and few criminals escape them, even if they have to be hunted for years over the length and breadth of the country. They move about with grave faces, and their flat hats and red tunics set off their tall athletic figures to perfection.

The Hudson's Bay Company, which is rooted in the past as we have seen, now has its headquarters at Beaver House in London. It still has trading posts all over Canada and in the Arctic. It sells no liquor to Indians or to Eskimos. Their posts contain a Hudson's Bay Store where anything can be bought from sweets to socks, snow-shoes to buttons and needles. The Hudson's Bay blankets with coloured stripes are famous for their quality. Indians and Eskimos bringing in furs from their trap lines receive a lead token which entitles them to credit in the store. The Company look after their welfare and that of their families. The post managers in the Arctic are men of the type who can face loneliness and hardship, as their only contact with the outer world is the radio and the arrival of the " Nascopie," the Hudson's Bay ship which voyages from Montreal every June, making a tour of the Arctic posts. The " Nascopie " steams past the bastions of Quebec laden to the gunwale with stores of all kinds, and arrives back at Churchill bringing Eskimos who need medical treatment, post managers who are going on vacation, and bales of furs.

Sometimes a stout-hearted girl will travel from Montreal on the " Nascopie " to marry a post manager in the North. I remember sending a present to the newly-born baby of a post manager's wife in Arctic Bay, the baby being the most northerly white child in the British Empire.

The Hudson's Bay Company presented to Their Majesties on their visit to Winnipeg in 1939 the statutory tribute of the Company to the reigning sovereign : two black beaver skins and the heads of two elk. The Company has been a factor in the development of Canadian life and is a force of vital importance to the Canada of the present day.

3

The Indians in Canada have had a less fortunate fate than the Eskimos, for they have suffered from contact with the white man and have been obliged to face the shrinkage of their territory and to give up their favourite modes of life.

They are the wards of the Canadian Government, who have treated them with imagination, kindness and sympathy. But they belong to an older world, and find it (except in some cases) very hard to adapt themselves to the life of to-day. The men dress themselves in old flannel coats and trousers, and the women in faded and torn jumpers and skirts, which, with their untidy bobbed hair, gives them a slovenly look. They find it difficult to be either neat or clean, and an Indian village has the appearance of a Heath Robinson drawing. Everything is crooked that should be straight, the doors hang half off their hinges, and the chimney pots slant in every direction.

Only on ceremonial occasions, when they don the full Indian dress complete with a headdress of feathers, do they recapture something of their old barbaric magnificence. They make wonderful guides, and are the best conservers of wild life as they never over-trap or shoot too many wild animals, which the white man, if unchecked, is apt to do.

In the reserves in the wilder parts of Canada their way of life is much like that of their ancestors, and some tribes, such as, for instance, the Stoney Indians near Calgary, breed horses for the ranchers. They still carry on basket weaving and wood carving, but they have little originality in design, and if not carefully guided will reproduce modern patterns in the crudest of colours. Their traditional handicrafts were subtle in design and colour, but unfortunately contact with the white civilisation seems to have made them forget their earlier artistic cunning.

Their affairs are administered by the Indian Branch of the Department of Mines, and reserves have been set aside for bands of Indians all through Canada.

A FAMILY OF STONEY INDIANS ON A RESERVATION
Near Calgary, Alberta

They are given financial help, schools and hospital treatment, and also an agent, who is resident among them and acts as their friend and adviser. The popular idea that the Indians are a disappearing race is not supported by fact, as they increase slightly in numbers every year.

4

Canada has given a second home to many people of many different nationalities. There are, according to the 1931 census, more English people than Scots or Irish. There are emigrants from every European country, as well as from Japan and China. There are settlements of Ukrainians, Finns, Poles, Russians, Germans, Greeks, Scandinavians (including Danes, Icelanders, Norwegians and Swedes), Yugo-slavs, Czechs, Hungarians, Bulgarians, Rumanians, etc.

It is wonderful how well they settle, on the whole, into their new background. The Scandinavians and Ukrainians find the conditions of life not widely different from those in their own countries. They are not nonplussed by having to go into a forest and fell trees with which to build themselves a house, in the way that a settler from the British Isles might be (who would perhaps expect to find a neat cottage ready-made for him). The long winters are like their long winters at home, and they do not find the intense cold a hardship.

It takes a foreign settler some time before he becomes fluent in the English language. The children pick up English at school and often draw their parents

THE LUMBER CAMP—LIMBING
Woodcut by Clare Leighton

more closely into the life of the community. The influence of so many different nationalities has brought a variety of religions into Canada. There are many followers of the Orthodox Greek Church, and some sects with strange customs, like the Dukhobors, Mennenites, Hutterites and Mormons.

The Central Europeans and Scandinavians have brought their native art into Canada. They are encouraged to sing their songs and practise their handicrafts. There will come out of Western Canada, I am certain, an art which has a Central European background with a Canadian slant to it. I would give as an instance some exquisite linen mats in my possession, embroidered with a tall stall of Manitoba wheat by a Russian woman, which have the charm both of Europe and Canada. Music flourishes among the New Canadians and the world will hear much of their choirs and orchestras.

These people, who are helping to build up the Dominion of Canada, have a deep love for their new home and an abiding gratitude for the welcome they have received there.

5

Canada is rapidly developing her artistic side. Orchestras, French and English, play to large audiences. Her painters are alive to the magic of the winter

THE LUMBER CAMP—LANDING
Woodcut by Clare Leighton

landscape, and have been quick to see the beauty of the patterns made by the humps and ridges of snow with clumps of fir trees showing dark in the surrounding whiteness. Jackson makes great play with these winter patterns, taking a group of buildings, some half-submerged fences, with lines of distant hills in the background. Coborne and Hennessey have also produced some vivid winter scenes, composed round a sleigh driven by a farmer in a bright-coloured jersey. Gagnon's exquisite set of illustrations to " Maria Chapdelaine " shows the old habitant life of northern Quebec, and will be always, historically (as well as artistically) valuable when that mode of life has receded into the past. Emily Carr depicts the soft gloom of the British Columbian forests and the vivid grotesqueness of the totem poles. Grandmaison has to his credit some fine studies of the thin, hawk-faced Stoney Indians ; and Arthur Lismer of the loaded fishing boats in the Maritime Provinces.

Stephen Leacock is perhaps the best known name in literature. He is an admirable humorist, and his " Nonsense Novels " rank as a classic. Mazo de la Roche has created an admirable saga of the White Oaks family in which she tells delightfully of the way of life in an old house in Ontario. Audrey Alexandra Brown has delightful quality both in her lyric and narrative poems. Marius Barbeau brings the life of French Canada, old and new, vividly before our eyes. There are many other excellent writers who are depicting the Canadian scene and Canadian way of life in prose and poetry.

HEAD OF AN INDIAN SQUAW
Crayon drawing by N. de Grandmaison

Canadians have only one regular theatre (in Toronto), but the Little Theatre movement, sponsored by the Dominion Drama League, has gone through the length and breadth of the land. Drama groups put on plays, write plays, and make their own scenery and costumes. They meet yearly for festivals. Some of the Canadian plays are charming ; some most moving, as, for instance, that one written by the wife of a prairie farmer about the drought area in Saskatchewan from which she came, and acted by herself and her family. The drama movement is bound to develop and to become more and more important in the life of the Dominion as time goes on.

6

There is much to say about the Dominion of Canada which cannot be told in this brief essay. It is in some ways an unknown land. Americans are apt to cross the border in the summer complete with ski outfits, and to show a considerable ignorance about their neighbours to the north. English people

HEAD OF AN INDIAN CHIEF
Crayon drawing by N. de Grandmaison

sometimes appear to think that Canada chiefly consists of the Rockies and the Quints. This not unnaturally annoys Canadians, who think that their neighbours to the south and their kinsmen from the Mother Country should be better informed.

It is partly the vast size of Canada that is responsible, and many people think of the whole of Canada in the terms of the one province which they know something about. It takes time to realise its variety of scenery and population and to cease to be awed by its vast size. Americans often do not know that Canada is larger than their own country, while English people find it hard to cope with its immense scale after the smallness of the British Isles.

You can pelt people with statistics without much avail and tell them that Canada is the second largest gold producer in the world ; that the St. Lawrence drains a territory of 500,000 square miles, which contains half the fresh water in the world, and recite many other rapidly changing figures about the fur trade, fisheries and mining ; but it is the romantic side of a country which fires the imagination, and I should have wished to say so much more about

Canada as a romantic land. I should like to have described in detail the new National Park in British Columbia called the Tweedsmuir Reserve. It is a triangular piece of ground with its southern apex almost touching the Bella Coola river, and with an area of approximately three and a half million acres, or 5,400 square miles. I should like to have written more about the lovely Whitesail Mountains, the endless wild life, the woods, lakes and rivers, and their healing quality for the sportsman and traveller who wish to get away from the din of the cities ; and to have said more about Drumheller in Alberta, where the bones of a reconstructed dinosaur may be seen flattened against a hillside, and where trunks of petrified forest trees lie on sandy wastes amongst cactuses ; and the Queen Charlotte Islands with the tall, proud tribe of Haida Indians, and the bay where the sea lions play and catch fish ; and the tapping of the maple trees, and boiling of the maple sugar in the spring in the province of Quebec ; and the time-honoured custom by which the lives of the porcupines and loons are spared, for the porcupine makes a meal for anyone lost in the dense bush, and the cries of the loons lead the traveller to a lake where he can get water to drink ; and the thrill of sitting in a canoe while the guides steer you safely through the angry water.

I should also have liked to write of the wild flowers ; those spring flowers often concealed under dead leaves in the woods of Eastern Canada ; the Indian fireweed (willow herb) which spreads over miles of country in the West of Canada where there has been a forest fire ; the tall wild delphiniums in British Columbia ; the ditches filled with golden rod in the autumn ; the woods and hillsides covered by wild Michaelmas daisies in the provinces of Quebec and Ontario.

But lack of space prevents more than a passing reference to all these, and I can only express the hope that many people will go and seek out these things for themselves ; also that each visitor will stay long enough near some lake, forest or river, to make a close study of its special charm which time alone can reveal.